Why is the I

DATE DUE

Acknowledgments

To the following journals and anthologies where these poems first appeared, and to their editors, my thanks and appreciation:

ACM, Another Chicago Magazine: "in the instant"
Amerasia Journal: "rush hour"
Berkeley Poetry Review: "emerald world"
The Best American Poetry of 2002, "Trail," reprint from *jubilat.*
CutBank: "daguerreotype of sleep" and "overhearing water"
Fence: "elegy"; "out of order"
jubilat: "Trail"
The Kenyon Review: "why is the edge always windy?"
Manoa: A Pacific Journal of International Writing: "a tractor"; "footsteps";
        "ventriloquist"
New American Writing: "Three-Auricled Heart"
The North American Review: "embarkment"
Once Upon a Dream: The Vietnamese-American Experience (Kansas City: Andrews &
        McMeel, 1995): "Light and Seaweed" published in different form as "untitled"
Phoebe: "Accordion"
Quarterly West: "on the 22 bus going home"
Seneca Review: "Coast"; "On the Art of Discussion"
Verse: "coyote"
Vietnamese History Lessons Curriculum (high school, California): "Light and Seaweed"
published in different form as "tree."

I would like to thank my parents for their support over the years—from Saigon to Houston and all the stops along the way. I also want to thank Jane Miller, Boyer Rickel and W.S. di Piero for their creative and professional assistance and guidance. Further deep gratitude goes to the University of Arizona and Stanford University for fellowships that aided me in the completion of this book.

Many thanks to the Foundation Ledig-Rowohlt for the inspirational summer at The Château de Lavigny International Writers' Residence in Lavighy, Switzerland.

Why is the Edge Always Windy?

poems by *Mộng-Lan*

TUPELO PRESS
Dorset, Vermont

Why is the Edge Always Windy?
Copyright © 2005 by Mộng Lan
ISBN 13: 978-1-923195-28-6
ISBN 10: 1-932195-28-9
Printed in Canada

Library of Congress Control Number: 2005906436
First paperback edition, November 2005

Tupelo Press
PO Box 539, Dorset, Vermont 05251
802.366.8185   Fax 802.362.1883
editor@tupelopress.org   web www.tupelopress.org

Cover painting, *Mysticism* (watercolor, 2004) by Mộng Lan
Drawings, calligraphy and photograph by Mộng Lan

Cover & text design by Howard Klein

This project is supported in part by the National Endowment for the Arts

For J.A.

Table of Contents

1.

2.

3.

4.

1.

Emerald World

1

                            remember the future

as seagulls tumble from slit in stratus clouds

          men walk with eyes grown onto their buttocks
                        others have stomachs flat to sand
     a woman   breasts dangling white & vocal
    the ocean's octave heard
         crashing

               against breakwaters
       heard so often it isn't

2

     under the sea's umbrage
          touching everything in sight
   density springs
            from light & the elements
nothing less but the world at stake

Rush Hour

Hanoi, Vietnam

i walk across a surge of motorcycles grown onto bodies fifty dollar
Chinese bicycles truck horns smeared against houses blitz of wheels
waterless streets
head-balancing her basket the woman of bread

dust   movement of bodies sinking into

traffic a ripping bustle there is the frontier *(when trafficblood wanes   it
never stops   when people sleep   there is one who doesn't)*

a row of mirrors repeating lives barbers wait   watch the mold descend
bat's wings on cornices shack walls   hiss of cyclo drivers *"đi đâu em ơi"*
where are you going?

      around and around

~

         my parents walked

these streets some forty years ago

they frequented the same bookstores walked
                              around Hoàn Kiếm lake held hands
& ate roasted corn from street vendors
in 1996 the air has not changed
                              but the renaming of streets houses torn rebuilt

                              state-owned buildings beside citizen-owned
eateries
            the *Tháng 8* movie theater has never been so empty

a legless body on sidewalk concrete
                              fishboned in traffic's throat

Hanoi   the inertia of an hourglass

passing the Israeli embassy where they mourn the death of their prime
minister   i wonder am i walking fast enough?

                        birds' shadows descend on wet palms

                                                      wings flap

Embarkment

Hà Tây, Vietnam

one-legged man forgets himself

      arpeggio of dark

the fake ray bans he'd been trying to sell for weeks are still in his hands

      shiftywind shaft of straw movement in stones ashes lilting to

is he glad he hadn't sold that pair to see the sun better or the moon the darkness between

      behind sheets a journey impossible to exist as twilight forever

for seventy-five years fat rats scutter & sup on dog feces

      forever a person can live

the cone-hatted women mud-smirched men of the fields see ambered time

      and smooth underbellies of songs rise into mist

children inch out with buckets of mauve ink-water at the behest of teachers

      pale reed soaked in whispers

are told to look into the water to view the eclipse not the sun itself

      behind the image the imagination

workers wade in hay ears beyond the winded birds

      behind words the intent a distortion

sinewy arms dangling mouths eyes to another world smarting by the chant of their braced

      bodies summing the nature of existence a total eclipse

the one-legged man removes his glasses   squints

Overhearing Water

                                  ears pressed i listen
        the drowsy delta
           sea-salt deep in my nostrils

used for the morning & evening meals
                 water   pumped from the sewage the streets

                                      rush down legs
       & alleyways (rooms wet from thought)
                      clink against
        sodden sidewalks odored
               with my hair as i wash upon rising
          clothes washed   scrubbed
     sound of tubs
        agreeing in the sudsy hands
     of a woman   her willful children about her

i want to dream but i hear
        women pailing men pumping
                             ion luring ion
        electron repulsing electron   gurgling
         feet always wet faces hands

       winter comes
         we wash in the cold
      in doused nights
          seasick the straw mat a cat tramples at midnight

i want to breathe but what breath

19

a woman still washes her husband's & daughter's clothes
                                        wringing the clothes hushed

                between life & death
                                        i hear poured into round tubs
                        emptied choke
                                        of water   tub against concrete
                the woman rinses her hands & feet

                        between day & night
                                                sounds of gravity
                        at 5:30 the first person wakes
                to rinse her phlegm mouth
                        noise of work begins
                                        with an avalanche of insomnia
                        morning drunkenness slippers
        & mothers prodding their children to school   i see the wash of smoke & tv
                ash   radio
                                                music bellowing
                the seventies the eighties Brothers in Arms
                                        a dusky voice like a flower hanging
        & the girl downstairs begins to wash her endless
                                        ebony hair

                the walkway leading to the 22 families' houses
                                        rivulets roving
                        down roof
                concrete algae-green

                        overhearing water
                                        Hanoi's innards alchemize to jade

Light & Seaweed

                 having no money they fed on shriveled stars
                   that had fallen billions of years
           ago the suicide's soul she made a blanket
                         from its wool
             which kept them warm beyond belief

& inside the house they built
from hair thighs calves & shoulders
smooth stomachs longing to perspire
bleeding eyes & savant foreheads
they hung seaweed
curtains of light

                   where the sun hadn't touched
               the sand under whale shadows
                   bellowing black shapes
         they dazzled themselves with interstellar
                       dust rubbing
                  it over their bodies

          ~

the blind woman whose arms are veined
of ocean   hair fallen
shakes the family tree of its names fruits

Coast

1

what are ten or a hundred years
                        the blink
            the wait

            numb   a nail
                        diligent as wind
            scars tucked in your fists
    you cross
            the etched palm of the Pacific

the ocean a letter
            written over shore
                    unread shred by waves

2

your last *Têt*

walls fall like seasons' masks
shadows lean back and forth
like paper   drums roll
police sirens shrill   Buddhists head for pagodas
the minute it strikes midnight

Saigon pick-pockets
barefoot selling imitation cigarettes
dusty marketplaces   thick mamas
& svelte virgins at money boxes
immortal motorcycles exaggerate the air
of shrimp batter

the lines on your face
don't detail

3

her legs forced open

moving hands
ugly mouths

4

on the shore a walrus
head bitten off   barnacles
on its fins   a thirsty Caliban
what you've lived through you are
undercurrents ripe to capsize
everyone the boat   the dying
brother   clothes burnt to flag help
prisons forged your will

where we were
a terrain created
from the coast i see our birthplace at the horizon's
sleeve   a conscious pinpoint

you trekked the Pacific   Vietnam's
coasts   Los Angeles   San Francisco   San Jose   Seattle
cities rolled together
chain-smoked

5

you drag
                        your belongings along the coasts
your duffel bag   pair of jeans
        another shirt   rootless memory

a snail sculpts
        sand down the length of water

                                waves come

Keel of Earth's Axis

& to think that father's waterbuffalo days weren't fabricated   repeating
until legend the stories of youth

watery-eyed his childhood comrade acknowledges him

lightstreams dilate the paddy fields

a family name skips on tombstones toward horizon

where children play savagely   men & buffalos carry erections of straw

handing the land over to the children handing tombstones ashen heads they are
bodies without hands moralizing its rock nature giving
over its stony self

sound of broken earth keel of its axis

2.

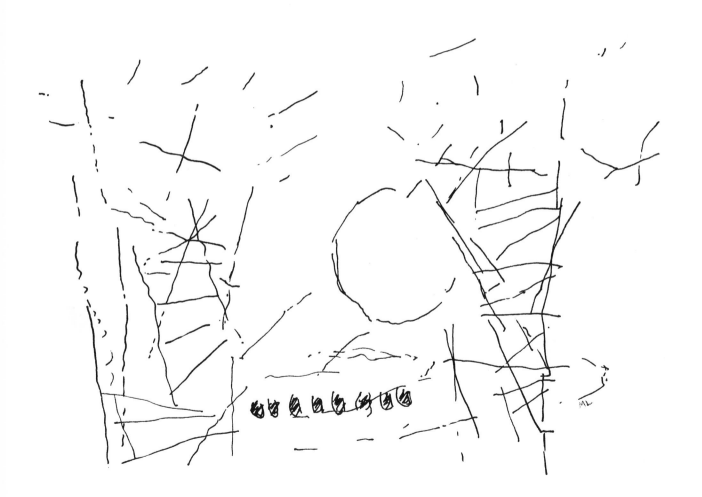

Daguerreotype of Sleep

where there's sleep
                        a cat cleaning herself
              or an idea of one
        thought enters the way
                        a person enters

                    before a line of one-handed mercury i stand
        wish the pages could be turned
        leave it untempered
                    its time has passed   its time passed

should i have stayed?
should've slept and laid my head on the table
                        a thousand white dresses   a million soarings of the heron
the wing of an orchid on my plate
& then i thought of the ordinary life

a handprint something made something forced
                                    something betrayed
                on a mountain range of mid winter
a slaughter   we're sleeping
a shirt full of laughter
                    your future in space
                            & a line   (it will not happen)

                                        a blue jay   an odor
                                          i suppose tonight is the end
a word with you is a season entire

alone go to the mountains

                        in an awkwardness
                          with no way out the spell of life
                                                take something

              we're not sleeping our hands
              wringing

Coyote

for hours wrestling in that panic
a boulder   fallen heads   an owl's hoot shoots across the valleys
                                                a stark vocation to call out night

there's no end   no myth
following sun into snake's hole

night falls & is greener   mountains like crenellated brains

chipmunk scatter dice rolled   lizards dash
under rock   flick

a boulder a large head fallen

                                        many of them have fallen

In the Instant

1

the man is found lying dead in the subway five hours
after his heart attack the place becomes cold & unclean   abode of flies

2

strength of water
                    extravagance of ocean & sun

moments   the smell of waves
are escapades embarkments & esplanades   long planks built for illusions &

tormentous skies   i breathe
& sleep   completely relaxed

no one else will do this for me   i must find
those extremes the friendships

i ride
the waves wake up to the desert blooming do you sense nothing but in

blueness? the sky is another ocean
in the desert   the sky tricks you into thinking it is water   so blue & clear

calm   waveless   & exhilaration?
my mind is free to explore color   largeness

3

on meat wrapped in banana leaves birds peck

                                      Saigon's foot is bound

the city   a person with amputated limb
                          has feet that strain for movement

4

sea insinuates   barge   edge & sail
    the lighthouse an eye flashing world

over the ocean's belly laughter sways
    at the feet of what is to come   at the foam of dis-ease

levity of men's guttural gambling   avalanches of household money
    flutter of cards   loss has a distinct beat

fire i build its wings search
    alley lights flood sand   stark

                                      capes draped over swellings

5

                                      year of the dragon
                                      souls fly downward free

6

pestle to mortar   my mother
   grinds wisteria blooms   waters
ashes in earthen jars   stethoscope
                    to garden   finger over thorn   instills

beats   i carry those wily rhythms   a species
   flitting within glass   waiting
to be forgotten   yet

chronicled   pulse of the mine-field   bursts of stone   "nothing but
   mines all the way" (in a Houston bar) the face a quiltwork
of skin taken from other parts
                    of the body sewn by a shaky seamstress

7

today in New York City it is
                    grey   even at summer's beginning
sirens everyday pitch their lights

O New York!

ghosts of America roam
land of fast food
                              joints defined by movement

herds of taxi cabs apartments too expensive to rent

trained hands typing digital lives

                                        commotion rust-shriek & blur of subway trains

        O New York!   until my legs detect a din i walk

(signs call me back)

                        shoes snivel   eyes a pocket

      wrinkled youth palsied
                                    elephantine ankles   cross-eyed ditty

a tic in the face is a chronicle of past grievings
                                                a cancerous cell love uncaved
i write into this handbook of daytime things   tantrums   & baby paraphernalia

        claiming words which gather time

answering life   i sit & stare into cracks stars of fate
i visit you
across the sea of
              disease between us

                                              let us be stricken
                                              with poems

O New York!

(2)

the flames   belligerent pieces   bodies flying

                                                    out of buildings
if not for gravity
                    pulling them down   the bodies would fly
                                directly to heaven

                        buzz of people
                bristling

an unexplainable breath   sucked
                    up from the sky   then suddenly the sky opens

                                spewing out all manner of things:

        a circus of hatred & abomination

                two airplanes spearing
the twin towers   exploding   melting

i work at Bellevue

        where next door is a temporary tented area   on 30th & 1st Ave

piles of

      bodies are carted there   arms   legs   heads

        identifiable only by DNA   such a stench i would like to forget!

patients & residents are ordered not to look

                out their windows

           for fear they would do something drastic   commit suicide

       being a doctor   i have to know   i have to look

Ventriloquist

what is there in this pungent darkness?

                                            notes drying on shelves

                   hollow mandolin

                         pinch of salt like stars

      there is no wine

                               ( )

      the world responds in resonances

this thing which wants to be more than that of mind

a signpost   a directory   a map   of human speech

            let's rewind the clock
                        whose hands flow into bodies

   where are you in this pythonine dream?
                   the air is denser than you

      walk & it sustains me
      i have no doubts the air also sustains me
             these voices deliquescent   unsustained glimmers

           ( )

      the first light is utterly different

to enter dislocated sleep

                                       loiter for the strain

                hung by the voice
                      til the throat dries

                           ( )

empty & quiet
          does the land speak
when one walks on it
                  when rain
                          blood drips from branches?

         toward a sky of broken plows

               there is the work to be done

A Tractor

squats waiting for its season
                              the steel hand
hungering night
                              music of crickets   whiskers resound
                wheat-walking fields
        hours of black rain
descend like cut hair   gnawing crevices moss & mucus
                              come alive
          awaken the clay

Out of Order

the hand a passport of the somnambulant

to go between this world & the next
for
what is

outlines are dishonest
during the hours
                            of a lifetime   consequences follow

these are what
i love stained glass of medieval
ages   vibrations of
holy places
my home a place
                            bulldozed by routine

what rises are undertones of the soul

                                         under soil   roots
                                       frazzled

that i love you is more inexplicable
than you think
you are
bamboo

Only This Life

1

only you are allowed to enter
voice for the first time
the look hesitant undemanding

body supple as sound
the hand unexpected   a fruit falling

skin curves of sand
lull below the arms
scent of the ocean's salt

2

the body pushed into life's mouth

3

velvet crunch
of white under feet   my heart

snowy lizards' tails
sleeping on branches
arms rhyme
with bending earth

a shadow slants
like a calligrapher's quill

4

pass the threshold

5

a genus of the solitary
                    the knitted
night   stained-glass boxes
                 where memories ferment
             unplanned you come

6

saguaros crack   monsoons

                          consider erosion of rocks

water's fire   lit

        worlds intersect   dusk   purity of ascent

ferocious nose of a cat
                    incandescent   through forces

        stay up waiting

                    planes converge   fates intersect

7

how long does a measure last?

8

sea in the sky
                              knives
              striking obliquely   army of light
                                   beating walls
                   the aquamarine houses are ghosts
                                        between crystal trees
              water steals over skewed floors

only this life

9

a cat sleeps one eye opened

On the Art of Discussion

1

always this autumnal music a rumbling internal scratchings of organs melodies of the ironing board we are stretching we go over bridges we cut through mountains searching for wheat and rice diamonds of the earth unraveling stories we go hearing crickets move under their lyric pretenses and of course the ghosts in delirious brawl and the return was inevitable for the goddess sleeps in all things even in the broom which sweeps lies.

2

listen
dew drops   earth turns   night sleeps for once
the lie puts a fork into our bodies   the lie is a viscous substance   is it truth
we are after   or a reflection of ourselves? i see the negative of myself burn
white under long silences

negatives of feet vendettas run   the lie a creature descending keep us close

keep us closed

3

with my hands i break it in half

listen   dew is born of the rift night & day   a fork between parts   sum
of twilight   waters these rocks egg of earth

the lie oils daily motions though it may smell like burning hair
            bring in the lakes
                              which go forever!

4

earth asleep for once   no cars no monsoons no insistence from the landlady to pay the
rent   but insistence from the landscape to make something of this enduring   to trip and play
hopscotch with pebbles and stones   tripping over the lines that come alive   actually   this
note was found in the hands of a little girl digging dirt   she loved to dig   and dug until
her fingers

47

5

adjust the weight of hours & days around the waist

6

where the mirage
is definitely a lie
the Tohono O'odom slumps a response to technology though overhearing
the idiom of the deceased   high-heeled shoes of nightmares
tussled odors of armpits   a shadow swastika of salamanders geckos

prays the tooth of dreams to come out   rains to flower from clouds
stars in the way tumble onto desert

7

"Most of the things of this world are done by themselves: 'The fates find out a way.'"

8

think of this as adventure
mold smoothing
into cheese   curling your hands around the iron bars

because we are weak & like to deceive ourselves we lie we lie from honor to save face the ghost to preserve honor beyond the grave we tell stories in order to lie

though the little girl grew up   she led an impossible life living in run-down
San Francisco hotels
                    under bats'
        wings
watching the junkies   she thinks   leave   leave

9

i dine alone on a train to the coast   let Buddha enter

sift the lies from sadness apart we will never weave
destinies from each other

the days are blissful   in repose   or supposed to be

note, section 7: Montaigne quoting Virgil, "Of the Art of Discussion."

3.

Pen & Ink

emptiness filled with water

              throwing one against the wall

oneself   no harbor

              hair-plugged   toilets tubes fractured

bleeds through doors

              of nails leaves   antlers

to find a way out of the labyrinth

              a mind without parents

an instant from which you free fall

life enters

              pulling a tendon

Accordion

1

                       mañana flies like molted feathers
      above the balmy earth
you watch
     heads purple spiked points the muralists the flashers idlers
         the mariachis' stroll   heart of trumpets

          wind throbs fragile
      under armpits

    Mission Street a mood of gypsy cats prowling

2

crack addicts tango
                 the sly feet
                          measured hand reaching for pocket

there's the hidden motion

                                             clear as a ghost

            a hand trick holding knife
in the dust of memory   you fight to go

                          back to a simple world of unembroidered desires

women their liquid eyes turn heads
babies protected with vinyl & Spanish   language cooling the soul firing intestines

        hidden motion   between knife edge & shadow

                    residue of chlorophyll   of
          night expert on insomnia
                          stretching its feet into bars

3

the man's face gouged by sun traffic & lust
                        la consejera Madalena snatches palms
                  for ten dollars projects a love a future

        "dingy as Saigon"

desire's anatomy: in thinking of what might happen
                                    during doesn't exist

4

O gelatinous night
of the pothead's coughing
romance clings to black hair

do you see the stricken men
the addicted ladies?

except for the feral cats
breeding in the backyard the house is barren

see that the cat's form is not what is   but attention
perched   waiting to strike

5

clear tap tap like ants in unison
        feeds the fungus caves in walls   a day comes
       you put out your hand
                    nothing screams
      cracks where rain had slept

branches like octopus arms
            wrangle the brisk cold   ocean days
       clothes to the laundromat
    over scraggy sidewalk   past
          the "El Niño" exhibition
       a century
     of rain falls

6

accordion time
surges on Mission Street
not even stopping for the Mayan goddesses
muralists are painting
a spray-canned
sun   fluorescent underwater canyons
gypsies linger   rain sows
air   pellets of memory
you scale
the wall   towards painted sun

watch the days rewind

[San Francisco, 1997]

Elegy

& what if hope crashes through the door what if

that lasts a somersault?

hope for serendipity

even if a series of meals were all between us

even if the aeons lined up out

of order

what are years if not measured by trees

Three-Auricled Heart

1

a clock tower
there is nothing around   but houses
monochrome dusk & mist
as if in a black & white film
a man counts down

because the waves
of Zepolite *(el lugar de la muerte)*
the feisty waters of Nha Trang
choked on their turquoise
carrying me away their mercuric arms
because the shards experience
metallic pieces
are miniscule worlds desolate
because that first slip into the world
the second & the third
glitched on an opaque membrane
has for its substance   patience
we shovel against the densest part of earth
chocking up iron   ions Icons
desiring the body
until the spirit is felt

2

births & deaths schlepped
on my back   trinkets
of the Fool   the Buddha
(in front of me   a jade sculpture
my mother's)   spews
out his thoughts
ensnared in my throat like a catfish
with enormous whiskers

the Golden Gate Bridge from my window
is a red of smothered crabs
cooked in dreamfog
savage-haired
drummers in the park   beat on
African rhythms cunning
bodies seducing

3

catfish dissected: in Tenderloin, a baby ruptures its own three-auricled heart
with a pair of rusty scissors the heart is found lying on stairway ledge next to pair
of scissors. bits of its twitching muscle clings to corridor. baby is carried
in hands of uncle, buried half-alive.

dream-stricken hand
                              my hair pushed back
          the nightmare wind
                         deep in my skin

              King Lear is Prospero
       by gregarious wind

          glass   cracked spontaneously
                                 broken shard tattling
     to floor   the distraught season
                               white voices
              embers of utterances

4

Kant's clock tower hovering a space of no time

the city is split in half a geode of skyscrapers

weeds have grown legs sprawling over highways

fossil vortex and your vices

splayed over the walls of the room

hint of magnolias splurge of daisies

for a while then ashes dispersed

what is left what is this season a name your nemesis

death and the scent of a particular

5

the seas dry up

leaving fossilized fish   salt diamonds

                                    then do we withdraw from life

            leave no trace

our breaths' embroidered

                        design   hardly cryptic

        whole lifetimes

                    laid full   bare

a camel's humped back

                            fragments sated with voices

On the 22 Bus Going Home

(scent of pain
                    painting houses all day i don't talk)

    the phone rings brings a voice dislocated
                                        without form or desire

you're plastic
            the phone tells you what to say how to touch

    in their urgency   suicides talk little
                            time spreads out color of jam

bus rides to dreams at point zero
                        houses zip by bleed

                                        a Moroccan man leans
    forth to show a vial of perfume from his country
                            its trees & earth encapsulated

Why is the Edge Always Windy?

at Phromthep Cape   the edge of the world   my dress unloosened
                   wind ripped along the coast   drove along until it lifted
       & we drove on jeep
                          around the roar's extremities

                        ( )

             the Thai curry   deepfried crab meat at Baan Rim Pa
                   sweet mint sauces
        hung to our clothes as did rain
lawless waves clinging to cliff

long tailed boats tear
the Andaman sea with their unmuffled motors
soggy newspapers sopped up night's moisture
clothes don't dry here & matches don't catch   only you were willing

( )

i had lost a day coming to Bangkok
"love shacks"   "up to you" cafes
another life
gained

            Paris   St. Germain des Prés   Rue Jacob   your reflection
on glass door walking toward me
                                          through garden archway—
never such a beautiful sight!

                                              (   )

            to the Louvre   the *bouqinistes*
                                    we went   tired & drunk from love
                              in the late mornings
            this sub-terranean language

       like discovering the hidden rooms in an old château
we find our loves
                               —what i see
      vastness and always water

                          (   )

silvery reflection of sky   teal Jura mountains
water oozed   aqua laving over
how could i ask anything of you?
                        raining   the rose opens

can life be passed when life is offered?
         the vine will search the

                                                            divine   quiet vineyards
                 roll in angles   grapes green & deep red

                                           (   )

                        this opal rain on linden trees   sunflowers
                                         if i could bottle your voice
                 dappling mountains near church steeple & Romanesque rotunda of Lavigny—
                 did you call me this morning or was it a dream?

mother & child take shelter under church porch
                    clouds blanket the Jura mountains near Geneva
                                    disappearing into light
                    did you come to kiss me?

                                    (   )

listen   the wind through grape crevices

& leaves

like waves upset fibers tangled repeating

octaves tongues perched

shaped in swan-light bodies float
on Lac Léman at Buchillon.
i lie on rocks glowing as your chest
& hear water's memory

( )

les deux baigneurs frolic on surf board
algae legs dangling in water
it seemed a promise
the beach everyday unmitigated

                                                    lost   a black silk sweater
in Phnom Penh   riding on motorcycle   driver in front
        you behind   your arms around me   darkness
& dust of the party-goers folding us   —where are you now?

                                        (   )

                    a pigeon windless
whaled up on my patio door
                        a wingless bird carrying
                                    unopened   wind-knocking door

4.

Trail

prelude

        this age our era i can correctly say this an era of exile
this satiny desert
on this trail of a thousand years there is us amidst misfits & assiduous trees

we have walked
over sand sick with evening of words spilling

          what is the remedy for momentum for mania a deciduous heart?
loitering now i speak of nothing no ideas just Vietnam motherland inside us
      & between us the air   Arizona sun magnanimous accepting everything

an ear of deaths in a polaroid photo & the killing
this age of hyper awareness this time of blue moons

         the ocean   past we touch
           inside our skin a sterling sound

we who have walked alone will no longer
through woods red with evening of dreams spilling
growing old a California sequoia green &
       sage as the saguaro branching

1

a crab crawls sideways into a polaroid photo tangled you loiter & now you speak of nothing
no ideas pushed into hole the fabric mice-chewed

you have been going back & forth from the border of . . . what was it?
when upon seeing a person with alzheimer's on tv when a flippant offer of someone buying
you something when after a family dinner in which the main conversation was having desires
versus shutting them off you wander into the streets eyes wet while you notice how roseate
the sky is how demure the heat is not its usual how you should be enjoying such a night but
nevertheless you go wherever your blind feet take you places well-acquainted see cars pass
& wonder if the headlights expose & wonder if any will stop

2

wild-eyed
next to your border a different dialect spoken
                    in the corridor your fingers pressed

listening monk this laughing Buddha belly & shoulders twitter a gurgle of ears listening
pressed to palm
                                    when the mood strikes

            strike!
                                    when i begin
                    & drown in salt
                        the Buddha's my own or Lao Tsze's in this mesmer
        following the folds in robe

a boy dies saving another from suicide
on the suicide isle are mist gargantuan in deceptions

            words spilled the throat a babe on motorcycle rolls onto street

3

to accelerate time i walk from Arizona to Texas to New York to
Vietnam

most content while making forgetting that night is night
(rug cat hair crumb)
& day day   this life is
to be in process is an act
of survival
follow the ends its awakened curves

through sterile passages of supermarkets i walk & walk
to contend with time then suddenly lack
slowness   then speed a velocity problem

silver butterfly heavy

inside this drift split

4

"within 100 years of contact with western
civilization, the Amazon tribes become extinct"

news lurking
not even metal smithing nor the even-marking tires
the soles of defunct shoes
a blandness narrative can't obliterate

world news worsens these days
                                 & you are not in my em-
brace

        the axis spinning is why we don't fall off haunting earth
i haunt the earth
                      looking
        for a phone this machine which allows us to be a-
                                             part
        how many digits is the number
                          for consciousness the total for God?

no one knows me wandering in this flesh
over the desert-feet soles of those i will never know
i am eager for the packed streets the embroiled pavements i wander in books finding myself
in paths that lead nowhere
                      but to designs in nature

i rove through strip malls grocery aisles of stuff cans & cans of songs looking loitering &
don't buy except
        what i need

                      (the everpresent Present the future it is here)
                a fault line the world grins
            & yet this hand full of epiphanies
                    minds that cannot escape nonchalance

5

(Chiapas)

           faces bought
           from a witch doctor
           carved stone of desolation
           shrines to the past (it is here)

a high turn of sea of sun
           & from this black jade survival

gone to the market fed there a life led there entrails bowls of bowels eaten
           meat meat & through stalls the tents striped with humor & flirtation

& men jerking off do you ever get sick of this?
           they do it with a life's content
      of blossoms / ever the orange flowers drowning

see the spiders spinning   caterpillars
           sheets of blisters ricocheting off surf
                  Aztec blood of Zapatistas

6

not for the cantilever of arguments
nor the cumulus remarks
                    the confused odor of tolerable American lives
nor the razor the vein nor for the contrapuntal snare do i come

but for the desert raging on a contact sheet the outbreak of pneumonia
                                        awkwardness of grand pianos
nonchalant pursuers of the dream the content hackers

i dream of sand dunes flying ridges & sun i dream of wind blowing darkly usurping cultural
designs   a liar in a tiger's den

in this city a blissful terror of invisible spires
cryptic skies talk less & less

                                        with my mother's hand
                                        i tether jade to the skin of books

shoring over names of friends who have left the last rite
i carve our faces on stone

            ((disclose with a kayak in throat))

7

what noises are harbored in these chained boats?
sometimes these moments alone from wood pulp bleached
these thoughts
are belligerent
old women
i will be incoherent with them

8

my neighbors push
shopping
carts
home

9

Amazonians on bare feet wooden dollies adorning their lips
women on New York streets high-heeled & aching

dreams of Arizona: there are abscesses
        households trying to make ends meet
                                                    dryness & trails
                    in heat people come out at night like lizards
                                        watch each other rodents slither
                    the gila monster ecstatic

drawbridges dams impermeable we have our historical delusions try to live one day

10

this soil of extremes
a throb of mice in walls
assiduous trees a moon-shaped sickle
a dossier of stillness

see this aerial view
a body of shimmering water copies the blazing desert
water & some moon

twisted orifices of mountains
passing clouds shape of trees
waiting to see you i write this song on the plains
on spent mountains

try to sleep but words float up
what do animals do when they're alone?
they claw themselves til the blood flows (animals
we're fine in motion)

this is what time does to you
& clouds pass their leaves

a snowflake fissured on window
patterned below the scandent mountains
they've had a million years to practice their lines